ACTS

TO THE ENDS OF THE EARTH

10 Publishing
a division of 10 of those.com

David Cook

50 UNDATED DEVOTIONS
THROUGH THE BOOK OF ACTS

Luke is the author of Luke's Gospel and the book of Acts. Today's verses provide the bridge between the two volumes.

In Luke 24:46–47, Jesus summarizes the purpose of God. Notice that verse 46 is a good summary of the Gospel of Luke – the suffering, the death and resurrection of the Christ. Verse 47 is a good summary of Acts – that same gospel being preached to the ends of the earth. Notice that verse 47 is as much the purpose of God as verse 46; the broadcast of the gospel, mission and evangelism is at the very heart of God's ongoing purpose until His Son returns.

Acts 1:8 is a similar verse to Luke 24:47. It sets the pattern for the unfolding narrative of Acts. The Holy Spirit will come on the church to empower it for witness in ever-widening circles until the gospel reaches the ends of the earth.

This tells us that Luke's purpose, under God, in writing Acts is to show the triumphant progress of the gospel, through Judea, into Samaria, throughout Asia, into Europe and finally to Rome. However, this is not triumphalism, for the gospel messenger will be opposed, tortured, imprisoned and martyred. There will be opposition from the outside religious and commercial interests and even dissension within the church, yet the gospel will progress and people will come to Christ. God buries His messengers but not His message.

Luke, in the original Greek, concludes his account in Acts 28:31 with the word 'unhinderedly'. The march of the gospel is ongoing; it has not yet ceased.

The book of Acts provides the church of the twenty-first century with its mandate – and your mandate for today. You have the Holy Spirit. He will empower you today for witness to Christ in a lost world.

'All hope in ministry lies in the Spirit of God operating on the spirit of men.' C.H. Spurgeon.[1]

REFLECTION

Think of the people you contact and of your witness to them. How can it be more effective? Do you think we make Luke 24:47 of lesser importance than Luke 24:46? What effect does this have on the church?

The opening two verses are very similar to Luke's introduction to his Gospel (Luke 1:1–4). Both verses are addressed to Theophilus, and Acts takes up where the Gospel left off – that is, with the resurrection of Jesus.

In verses 4 to 8, Luke records Jesus' final words to His disciples before He ascends to His Father. The disciples' question in verse 6 is a natural one. As resurrected Messiah, will Jesus now bring down the curtain of history, restore Israel to her rightful place and reign over all creation? Jesus makes it clear that before this happens there is more to be done, but it is not merely human work, it is Spirit-empowered witness.

So they are to wait (v. 4) and they will receive power (v. 8). This is the gift of God to His people of which John was speaking (v. 5) – the baptism of the Holy Spirit. The effect of this baptism is that the Holy Spirit will enable the church in its witness. Your witness today is one part of a two-part witness. You witness. But as you do, the Holy Spirit also witnesses with you (see John 15:26,27).

Jesus then ascends to the right hand of the Father (v. 9). The proof of this, says Peter, is the outpouring of the Holy Spirit (Acts 2:32,33). The disciples are reminded that just as Jesus has gone up, so He will come down. These heavenly messengers, similar to those who announced the resurrection (Luke 24:4), also now remind the church that there is a limited time to work, until Jesus returns (vv. 10,11).

Jesus spoke of His ascension in Luke 22:69. His resurrection was the means to His ascension, and His ascension means His total exaltation to the right hand of God, where He intercedes for us (Rom. 8:34). He now occupies the highest place (Phil. 2:9), He bestows gifts to His people (Eph. 4:11), and from the place of exaltation He will return in triumph to bring in the new heaven and the new earth.

It is little wonder that Paul encourages us to set our hearts and minds on the things above where Christ is seated at God's right hand (Col. 3:1–3).

REFLECTION

Think of the ways that Christ's ascension can be a source of blessing for you. What is He doing at the Father's right hand? What do you think the ascension meant to the Lord Jesus? What are you to be doing with the gifts He has given you until He returns?

After the final separation of Jesus from His disciples, now numbering about one hundred and twenty (Acts 1 v. 15), one would expect gloom to set in. But no, we find the Christians going about their business. They return to Jerusalem where Jesus tells them they are to wait for the gift of God (Acts 1 v. 4) and they set themselves to pray earnestly (v. 14).

Peter seems now to be the acknowledged leader and spokesman for the group. He sees, in the betrayal of Christ by Judas and the selection of a replacement for him among the apostles, a fulfilment of Psalm 69:25 and Psalm 109:8. To qualify for selection, a man must have been with the apostles from the time John was baptizing up to the ascension of Jesus, and his central task is to be a witness to the resurrection. Two men are proposed, prayer is offered for guidance, lots are cast and Matthias is added to the eleven apostles.

Why does Luke include this detail? Why not move from the ascension straight to Pentecost? After all, Matthias is not mentioned again in the book. Judas's betrayal was a major failure of leadership that needs to be acknowledged and rectified. Luke tells us in some detail of the failure of Judas because he is providing a 'warts and all' coverage of the history of the church. He does not idealize the church; he recognizes the hypocrisy of Ananias and Sapphira in chapter 5, the bickering of the widows in chapter 6, Peter's behaviour in chapter 10, and even Paul's impatience with John Mark in chapter 15.

'The best of men are men at best.' We are to recognize our own frailty, and Luke shows the church facing up to the need to renew its leadership following the apostasy of one of the apostles. Damage had been done and restoration was required. The church did not then, and must not today, try to simply cover its sin; sin needs to be acknowledged and dealt with.

In an atmosphere of prayer, Peter sets out the necessary criteria, the lot is cast and Matthias is the choice. The apostolate is now complete once more and its key function (v. 22) is to witness to the reality of Christ's resurrection.

'See what the apostles were ordained to; not a secular dignity and dominion ... but to preach Christ and the power of His resurrection.' Matthew Henry on Acts 1:22.[2]

REFLECTION

In what ways does the early church provide a model for us concerning leadership selection? In what ways does Judas serve as a warning to you? See verse 17.

DAY 4   **READ** Acts 2:1–13

Pentecost (meaning 'fifty') was one of the three great festivals of Judaism. Fifty days after the completion of the barley harvest, it was a time to give thanks to God for the completion of the harvest. Later, it came to commemorate the giving of the Law to Moses at Mount Sinai. The festival was all about fulfilment, completion and finality. It is most fitting, then, that the Holy Spirit should be poured out on the church at this festival. His coming is the evidence that Christ is risen and has ascended to God's right hand; His work is now complete.

The coming of the Spirit is associated with the sound of wind (v. 2; cf. John 3:8) and the sight of fire (v. 3; cf. Exod. 3:2). The effect is that the 120 were filled with the Holy Spirit (v. 4; cf. Jer. 31:33, which anticipates this day) and they speak in tongues, so that the different language groups of verses 9 to 11 hear them disclosing the wonders of God in their own language. Luke records the range of responses – 'bewilderment' (v. 6), 'Utterly amazed' (v. 7), 'Amazed and perplexed' (v. 12), and mockery (v. 13).

We may argue about tongues here, but note that the recipients did not speak in inarticulate sounds. The word 'tongue' in verse 6 translates the original word 'dialect' and is in parallel with verse 11, where the word used is 'glossa' or tongue. The ideas are parallel – the 'tongue' here is a dialect; here are people speaking in dialects without having attended language school.

The focus of these verses is that God has come to live within His people, and the immediate effect of this is the reversal of the scrambling of languages that occurred with the building of the Tower of Babel (Gen. 11). The Holy Spirit has come upon the church, and He enables effective witness. He is the Spirit, after all, who Jesus said would empower for witness (Acts 1:8).

Matthew Henry says the significance of this event 'is to dignify and so to distinguish these men as messengers from heaven and therefore like Moses at the bush, the crowd will turn aside and see this great sight.'[3]

REFLECTION

How do you think the Holy Spirit helps you in your witness? What do you think wind, fire and tongues might symbolize about the Holy Spirit's ministry?

Whenever a crowd gathers in Acts, a believer takes the opportunity of preaching to it. Here is Peter, who a little earlier had denied Christ, now fearlessly and with crystal clarity preaching the gospel. The Day of Pentecost is the day in the church calendar when there is preaching on the Holy Spirit, but the Spirit is not the focus of Peter's address; rather, Jesus is. Peter speaks only of the Spirit in relation to Jesus.

The big idea of this Pentecostal sermon is that Jesus was crucified, was raised to life and is now exalted to God's right hand, and that Peter and the others are eyewitnesses of these events. Jesus was 'accredited by God' (v. 22), according to the 'set purpose' of God, was crucified (v. 23), and was raised from the dead. Death had no claim on Him because He had no sin (v. 24). The proof that He is exalted to God's right hand is that He now pours out the Holy Spirit (vv. 32–33). The summary is found in verse 36.

Peter's audience is Jewish. Therefore, he wants them to know they should not be surprised at these events because they fulfil what Joel predicted for the last days (vv. 17–21). In verses 25 to 28, Peter quotes David in Psalm 16. The words of v. 27 are extravagant – Peter says David did not use these words of himself but of one greater than David who 'will not be abandoned to the grave'. The Old Testament is Peter's reference point for the Jewish audience.

Notice also that Peter does not hesitate to be direct. In verses 23 to 24, he makes the clearest contrast between what they did to the Son in God's name – 'put him to death', and what God Himself did – 'raised him from the dead'. The response to this sermon was deep conviction (v. 37). Peter tells them they are to repent and give public witness to their repentance through baptism (v. 38). The Christian gospel involves take and give (v. 38). God *takes* our sin and deals with it, and then *gives* us His Holy Spirit. This is the ongoing offer to all those who repent and turn to Christ.

That day 3,000 accepted the message (v. 41).

REFLECTION

Think about the twin blessings of forgiveness and the Holy Spirit in your life, and be thankful. In verse 40, Luke describes Peter as warning the crowd. Are we serious enough in sharing the gospel with others? When was the last time you were warned not to neglect the gospel's promises and warnings? The apostles could say, 'We are witnesses' of the resurrection and the ascension. What can we say today?

One of the features of our modern culture is our intense population density, yet we lack togetherness. We have proximity without community.

In these verses, we read of the community life of the prototype church. They shared the common experience of hearing the gospel, repentance and baptism, and now they shared a common devotion. (The idea of the word is attachment like glue.) They stuck to the apostolic teaching and to the community and the breaking of bread. (The 'breaking of bread' may indicate the Lord's Supper or hospitality and prayer – see verse 46.)

Jesus had prayed in John 17:23 for the complete unity of believers. We now see this deep unity built around a common experience and common devotion.

This even extended to a Spirit-motivated voluntary socialism (vv. 44,45). We may think that the church was fairly self-absorbed, but no, their pooling of resources was to meet human need. At a time when government was not concerned for social welfare and life was cut-throat and cheap, no wonder people were impressed with this new society growing up in their midst in Jerusalem 'enjoying the favour of all the people' (v. 47).

Again Luke reminds us that this impressive community is not just a matter of people turning over a new leaf, but is superintended by God (v. 43). God enabled the apostles to do wonders and 'the Lord added to their number' (v. 47). This is God at work through the life and witness of His people.

The church is never to be a closed, secret and introverted community. All true fellowship is founded upon and focused on the gospel. All true fellowship overflows into evangelism which, after all, is the overarching mandate of the church (Acts 1:8).

You need such a fellowship with your fellow believers. The fractured world needs to see church communities witnessing to the reality of substantially restored human relationships because of the gospel.

REFLECTION

How can you encourage your local fellowship to be more like its prototype?

Note how often community words are used in verses 42 to 47. How does this church challenge our unhealthy individualism?

 **DAY 7** **READ** Acts 3:1–10

Many 'miraculous signs were done by the apostles' (Acts 2:43). Here is one of them.

In such a dynamic book which shows the gospel 'on the way', it is ironic that the first sign should concern an immobile man. This man was obviously totally dependent, having to be carried to the Temple to beg. Another irony is that a man in such desperate need should be placed at the gate called Beautiful (v. 2). He was now over 40 years old (Acts 4:22) and he had been crippled since birth (v. 2). All the world could do for him was to throw a few coins his way. Peter and John, however, were clear that the church could do far more.

Peter has no coins to give him. Rather, he calls on him in the name of Jesus Christ of Nazareth to walk (v. 6). The response is instantaneous. It is not that he got better gradually; his feet and ankles immediately became strong so that he went 'walking and jumping' (vv. 7,8). This is an incredible creation miracle, removing the cause of paralysis and bringing muscle to existence. Even the Sanhedrin could not deny the reality of 'an outstanding miracle' (Acts 4:16).

It is clear that just as God had accredited Jesus by miracles and signs (Acts 2:22) so He is now accrediting the apostles, and therefore their message, in the same way (Acts 14:3). Periods of fresh revelation in Scripture are always accompanied by authenticating signs.

The crowd is 'filled with wonder and amazement' (v. 10). Peter takes the opportunity afforded by the gathering of a crowd to preach the gospel to them. The church is mandated to preach the gospel. The sign both draws a crowd to hear the gospel and authenticates the message.

Peter, the source of Mark's Gospel, would have remembered Jesus' words from Mark 1:38 when the crowd was looking for Him to heal, that He had come to preach: 'That is why I have come.' The healing of the man was a means of solving his deeper need as well as that of the crowd – to become eternally healthy.

REFLECTION

In what ways is the beggar's physical experience symbolic of our spiritual experience? Is there ground here to think that the church's mandate is to preach and physically heal?

One distinctive feature about the preaching of the apostles is their obvious self-effacement. The politicians such as Herod may bask in self-glorification with disastrous results (Acts 12:21–23), but the apostles are the very opposite (Acts 14:11–15). The apostles are not gurus seeking the limelight and the acclamation of the crowds. So Peter makes it clear it is not because of his and John's power or godliness that the cripple walks, it is because of Jesus (v. 16).

Again, a clear distinction is stated between how the Jews treated Jesus in the name of the God of Abraham, Isaac and Jacob – they disowned (vv. 13,14) and killed Him (v. 15), and how God treated Jesus – God glorified Him (v. 13) and raised Him (v. 15), and the apostles were eyewitnesses to this. Peter calls for a response in verses 17 to 26, showing the strong Jewish heritage of the Christ and that what has happened is in fulfilment of the Old Testament Scriptures (see v. 18; vv. 21–25). All have a strong element of fulfilment.

God is in control. God is working out His purposes. Therefore the Jewish crowd is to repent, for they have the privilege of being heirs to the promises of God (v. 25), and their repentance will bring about forgiveness and times of refreshing including, in Peter's mind, the return of the Christ as He had promised (vv. 19,20). Christ's return from heaven will be the ultimate fulfilment of God's promises to restore all things at His coming (v. 21).

Peter sees Jesus as the fulfilment of God's promises to Moses in Deuteronomy 18:15–19:

- like Moses, Jesus is from among their own;
- God will put His words in Jesus' mouth;
- disobedience to Jesus' words will be called to account.

Jesus is the prophet who not only speaks God's words but *is* God's Word (John 1:14,18). When Jesus speaks, God speaks. When Jesus acts, God acts. In Jesus' attitudes, we see the attitudes of God.

The healing of a crippled beggar is God accrediting His Son and His words. It is little wonder that Israel should repent of their disobedience and their treatment of Him – as should we.

REFLECTION

How much is ongoing repentance towards God part of your daily experience? How does apostolic self-effacement challenge self-exalting spiritual leadership?

The world is no friend of the church. Today we meet a theme in Acts which will repeat itself throughout the book – opposition.

The concern of the Jewish hierarchy is seen in verse 2, the 'proclaiming in Jesus the resurrection of the dead'. Luke is quick to remind us that, in spite of opposition, the gospel continues on its all-conquering way (v. 4). The same people involved in the crucifixion of Jesus now question Peter and John as to how they performed this miracle (vv. 5–7).

Peter is both clear and courageous in his answer. It is Jesus who is responsible for the miracle (v. 10) – 'You crucified Him, but God raised Him from the dead' – and this was to fulfil Psalm 118:22 that the one rejected would ultimately triumph (v. 11).

Here again is the familiar pattern of evangelism to the Jewish audience:

- the contrast of what you did in the name of God and what God did;

- the death and resurrection of Jesus;

- the fulfilment of the Scriptures.

Acts 4:12 is a timely reminder to us of the uniqueness of Christ. There is no other who can save – 'no one else ... no other name'. Such a verse makes it clear that Christianity is not one way among many ways to God. If the Christian faith is true, then all the other faiths must be false because there 'is no other name'. The basis of such a claim is that He is the one who died, was raised and was exalted to God's right hand. Further proof as to the reality of the claim is the crippled beggar standing healed before them. The ascended Christ is still active.

When John the Baptist doubted whether Jesus was the Christ, he asked the right question (Matt. 11:3). 'Are you the one who is to come, or should we expect someone else?' If Jesus is not the way, or not the sole way, who else has done what He did? Should we still be looking for another? The answer of the gospel is, 'no one else ... no other name'.

Peter and John are accused, they are being interrogated, but they are not passive victims. They are on the front foot; they are on the attack with the gospel.

REFLECTION

Memorize Acts 4:12 and think about its implications for you, your friends, the world and evangelism.

How should you respond in the face of opposition to the gospel?

In John 7:15, the Jews were amazed that Jesus knew so much without ever having studied. In today's passage, the Jewish leaders are amazed at the courage of Peter and John and note that 'these men had been with Jesus' (v. 13).

We are amazed at the blindness of the Sanhedrin, that despite the clear evidence of the healing of the man and the claim that this was the work of Jesus, they think they can stop the gospel by moving a motion in the assembly that there should be no more Jesus talk (v. 17). There is no rational debate or presentation of contrary evidence, merely this response – 'Stop this talk.' Somehow they thought this would change reality and everything would go back to the way it was. No way! Peter and John have been with Jesus. They had 'seen and heard' (v. 20). They were eyewitnesses of His resurrection and exaltation. They are under the authority of God, who is a far higher authority than the Sanhedrin (v. 19). They will repeat their testimony again in Acts 5:29. Let the highest court of Judaism decide – should God be obeyed, or a human court?

The Jews' own argument before the Roman courts was exactly this; their ultimate authority was no human court, but God alone. It was said of the Scottish reformer John Knox that he feared God so much that he had no fear to stand before any human tribunal.

Peter and John had the same conviction. They were witnesses, and they had been with Jesus. They were the leaders of a group of people mandated by God Himself to speak. 'We cannot help speaking' (v. 20) they say, and so they give us the ongoing model for our response to irrational, worldly opposition that seeks to silence our speaking of the gospel.

What the prophet heard, 'thus says the Lord', the apostles saw and heard, and so spoke. Today, we can say with equal confidence, 'Thus the Lord has written.' We have the historical written record of the revelation of God, and the accredited testimony of the prophets and the apostles, each of which focuses on the Lord Jesus. The more determined the world is to ignore us, the more determined we must be to speak.

REFLECTION

Think of the fear you might have for the tribunal compared with the fear you have for God. How could Peter and John have had such courage? In the face of such clear evidence, why is the Sanhedrin so blind?

The immediate response of the church to the threats of the chief priests and elders is to pray. They did not turn to political manoeuvring and they did not ask for safety. They prayed to the Sovereign Lord (v. 24), reminding themselves that it is God who is in control, not the Sanhedrin. They remind themselves that He is the creator. They remind themselves of the Scriptures, from Psalm 2, to the effect that humankind's raging and plotting against God's Anointed is in vain.

Again, in verse 27, they mention the human players but, once more, in verse 28, they put them in their place. Herod, Pontius Pilate, the Gentiles and the people of Israel did what God had decided beforehand should happen. As Joseph reminded his brothers in Genesis 50:20, 'You intended to harm me, but God intended it for good ...' Here is the crowning conviction of Romans 8:28 – that in all things, God works for the good of His people, and in all things God will take the evil intentions of people and use them to accomplish His purpose. The cross is the best example of that.

The mandate of the church is to speak the gospel, and the church prays that it would do so (vv. 29,30), that no threat will slow down the church in its ministry. Note again that they do not pray for safety, but for bold speech (v. 29) and accredited speech (v. 30). Luke records the shaking of the place and their filling with the Holy Spirit; the same people baptized in the Spirit in Acts 2 are now filled afresh with Him. We are baptized once, but filled with the Spirit often.

The fruit of filling is again underlined in verse 31 – bold speaking of the Word of God. The first resort of the church under threat of persecution is to pray about God's sovereign control; its petition is about bold speech; its result is spiritual fullness showing itself in bold gospel proclamation.

This is a great pattern for we who are under all kinds of threats to silence us today.

REFLECTION

How does this experience of the church show us the best way to face up to tough circumstances? Are you facing a similar situation today? If so, then write out a prayer like that of the first-century church and pray it in relation to your situation.

A gain, as in Acts 2:42–47, Luke gives us a glimpse of life in the early church, and what an impressive community it is.

Life in the first century was cheap. There was no welfare. People had only family networks, and if they failed they were on their own. The unity of the Christian community extended to possessions; they shared everything as if they were members of one family. The principle was one of equality. If someone was needy, their needs were met by the abundance of others (v. 34) and laid at the apostles' feet for distribution. Here, then, is a Spirit-inspired, voluntary socialism. Nikita Khrushchev once said that communism's failure was its failure to produce the selfless man. What the political system cannot do, God through the gospel of His Son can do. Here is a selfless, generous community of people of the new covenant.

Luke mentions one person as an example, Joseph of Cyprus. Renamed Barnabas, the son of encouragement, by the apostles, he did what was described in verses 34 and 35. True to his name, Barnabas introduces Saul to the apostles in Jerusalem (Acts 9:27). He is sent by the church in Jerusalem to encourage the Gentile church in Antioch (Acts 11:22). He seeks out Paul in Tarsus (Acts 11:25). He leads the first missionary journey with Paul (Acts 13:2). Paul soon becomes the dominant partner and Barnabas willingly plays second fiddle (Acts 13:42; 13:46; 14:1; 14:12). Barnabas was far more patient and generously minded towards Mark than was Paul (Acts 15:36–41). Barnabas is a great example of humility and generosity. He was a true disciple of the Christ, who came to serve (Mark 10:45).

I pray a daily prayer that God would give me a mind that is clean, generous and humble. Barnabas is a very good example of a life lived with such a mind. But Luke will not have us idealize the early church, because the generosity of Barnabas stands out in stark contrast to what is about to follow in chapter 5.

REFLECTION

What is it about Barnabas that gives you a model to follow? Do you think the principle of equality among God's people has relevance for today? How might this apply to believers with investment property, compared with believers struggling with a first mortgage, compared with believers who are renting?

DAY 13

READ Acts 5:1–11

Today we meet sin for the first time in the new covenant community.

Just as Israel entered the Promised Land and God showed them how seriously He takes sin among His own people with His judgement of Achan's sin (Josh. 7), so now God shows His new covenant community the unacceptability of sin.

God's judgement on Ananias (v. 5) and his wife, Sapphira (v. 10) was instantaneous. What they had done was devil-inspired (v. 3) and constituted lying to the Holy Spirit (v. 3), lying to God (v. 4) and testing the Spirit of the Lord (v. 9). What precisely was their sin? They had conspired together to sell a piece of property, like Barnabas, and lay only a portion of the sale price at the apostles' feet as if it were the whole amount. They wanted the reputation for generosity like Barnabas, while keeping back part of the money for themselves.

It was this deception that Peter highlights (v. 4). It was their land and they could have kept all the money for themselves, but they sought a reputation that was built on deception. They hypocritically wanted an undeserved reputation. Whether or not Ananias and Sapphira were true Christians is not answered, although

they were certainly part of the new covenant community. The judgement that resulted in their swift removal from the community was actually merciful of God, because it meant that their deception and hypocritical presence would not continue to plague the Christian church.

What an impression this must have made on the young men referred to in verses 6 and 10. They may have wondered when all this was going to stop. A primary sin of the religious leaders of Jesus' day (Matt. 23:2 ff.) was that of hypocrisy – teaching one thing yet doing another. It is this sin that enters the Christian community and is judged.

Beware of wearing a mask, of seeking a reputation that does not fit with the reality of your life.

REFLECTION

In what ways may hypocrisy show itself in your life today? Why might this incident, extreme as it seems, represent the mercy of God?

The ongoing growth of the church is inhibited neither by politicians' threats nor by internal hypocrisy.

Clearly God is accrediting His gospel message in miraculous ways (vv. 15,16). Luke now tells us that the motivation of the Sanhedrin is jealousy (v. 17), the same motivation behind their earlier attitude to Jesus. But prison is an ineffective weapon against the apostles. God's messengers cannot be stopped as long as He has work for them to do. The denial of responsibility for the death of Jesus by the Jewish authorities (v. 28) has a very familiar contemporary ring to it. Verses 29 to 32 are an excellent summary of the apostolic response. Note the following elements:

• God raised Jesus from the dead. 'You killed him on the tree';

• God exalted Jesus to His right hand that He might give repentance and forgiveness to Israel;

• we are witnesses of this and so is the Holy Spirit.

The response to such a message is similar to the response to Stephen's speech (Acts 7:54) and perhaps the apostles would have met Stephen's fate but for the wise intercession of Gamaliel (vv. 34–39). Gamaliel reminds the Sanhedrin of Theudas (v. 36) and Judas the Galilean (v. 37), who both appeared claiming to 'be someone', but later were killed, and their followers scattered.

Similarly, he says, let the apostles go, for their cause will fail if it is of human origin (v. 38), but if, on the other hand, it is of God, who can effectively oppose it?

The apostles were flogged, then released, but kept teaching and proclaiming, despite the Sanhedrin forbidding that activity. Saul/Paul, a student of Gamaliel, had no such open attitude to Christianity. He saw more clearly that the old system must stay, and therefore the new must be banished. According to the logic of Gamaliel, the ongoing growth of the church and its continuation to this day is ample evidence of its divine origin.

To oppose the gospel is to fight against God (v. 39) – surely a hopeless enterprise.

REFLECTION

Why did Gamaliel and Saul have such different attitudes to the new movement? Note the following: The high priest and his associates (v. 17), the captain of the guard and chief priests (vv. 24,26), the Sanhedrin (v. 33), the flogging and the silence ordered (v. 40). What do the opponents of the apostles have in common?

Luke continues with his realistic portrayal of the Christian community. At this stage, the early church consisted of believing Jews both from a Hebrew-speaking background as well as from a Greek-speaking background. The Greek-speaking Jews complained that their widows were being discriminated against in the daily distribution of the welfare, which favoured Hebrew-speaking widows.

In verse 2, the apostolic response is both swift and public. They recognize the priority of their own ministry, 'the word of God'. But they are not implying that ministry of the table (that is, distributing food) is beneath them, because they show that this is a ministry to be undertaken by men 'full of the Spirit and wisdom' (v. 3).

The apostles gladly delegate this serving ministry so that they can focus on prayer and the Word, which is their key ministry. The good is the enemy of the best. Thank God that the apostles recognized God's call to the best in their own ministry of the Word and prayer, and made sure that it was not disrupted by the good – that is, waiting on tables.

The whole community (v. 5) chose seven men who they set apart for this ministry (v. 6). In a community culturally divided like the early church, there is great sensitivity to the potential disruption which could flow from the complaint (v. 1) that the Greek-speaking widows were being overlooked. Seven men, all having Greek names, were chosen; not five Greek-speakers to two Hebrew-speakers, or four to three, but seven Greek-speakers to nil.

This shows the early church's determination 'to keep the unity of the Spirit through the bond of peace' (Eph. 4:3). The apostles' clear thinking and their commitment to this God-given unity is blessed by God. The result (v. 7) is the rapid increase of the church, with the gospel reaching deeply into Judaism and a large number of priests becoming obedient to the gospel. The gospel continues on its march to the ends of the earth. The threat of prison, and now internal complaining, do not frustrate its progress.

REFLECTION

What can we learn about handling disruptions in the local church by what the apostles do in this passage? How does the apostolic conviction, evidenced here, encourage you in your ministry?

The focus now shifts to one of the seven deacons who is described in verse 3 as 'full of the Spirit and wisdom' and in verse 8 as 'full of God's grace and power'.

Luke gives a great deal of space to Stephen because his martyrdom will be the catalyst (according to Acts 8:1 and 11:19 ff.) for the spread of the gospel to non-Jewish, Gentile territory. Greek-speaking Jews begin to argue with Stephen (v. 9) but, when they cannot better him in argument, they resort to underhanded ways. They persuade some men to make false allegations about him and have him brought before the Sanhedrin. The allegations (v. 11) are of blaspheming against Moses and God. This is elaborated on in verses 13 to 14 with the claim that Stephen speaks against the Law of Moses and says that the Temple will be destroyed.

In many ways the experience of Stephen parallels the experience of Jesus Christ; see the similar charge made against Jesus in Matthew 26:61 and Mark 14:57,58, and against Paul in Acts 21:28. The best false charges are those with an element of truth. Stephen probably did report Christ as speaking of the destruction of the Temple, meaning His body, and the fulfilment of the law, and in favour of the new covenant gospel.

Stephen's integrity and serenity are obvious (v. 15). He is now ready to answer the charges before the highest court of Judaism, the Sanhedrin. When reasoned debate fails (as in chapter 4 with the Sanhedrin, and chapter 6 with the Synagogue of the Freedmen), the world resorts either to the oppressive exercise of power in seeking to impose silence, or the desperate search for fake witnesses and charges.

We hold the truth. For the Christian, the best case for truth is made by its clear and open presentation. God is the great evangelist who blesses the clear proclamation of truth. Like Paul (2 Cor. 3:2), we renounce underhanded ways that seek to manipulate adherence to the gospel. These methods are unworthy of the gospel itself. Our trust is not in eloquence but in God to do His work through the gospel (1 Cor. 2:1). Neither is our interest in quelling the rights of others to proclaim their religion; truth has nothing to fear from its counterfeits.

The opposition of the world to the gospel is stubborn, irrational and perverse. In 2 Corinthians 4:4 the reason is clear. Like Stephen and Paul, our response must be to 'preach not ourselves, but Jesus Christ the Lord' (2 Cor. 4:5, KJV).

REFLECTION

How inevitable is opposition for the faithful Christian witness? How rational is the world's opposition to the gospel today? How does it respond underhandedly now?

Stephen's speech to the Sanhedrin falls into three sections:

1. vv. 2–16: the Patriarchs – Abraham, Isaac and Jacob.

2. vv. 17–43: Moses and the Law – in which he deals with the charge of blasphemy against Moses.

3. vv. 44–50: the Temple and the charge of blaspheming against God.

Stephen provides a review of Israel's history to show that Israel has always rejected God's messengers, culminating in the murder of God's righteous one (v. 52). It is similar to psalms 78 and 107:

• verses 2 to 16 recount the golden age of Israel and yet even here there is rejection of Joseph (vv. 9,10).

• verses 17 to 43 where Israel rejected Moses (vv. 27–29) and turned their back on him, making the golden calf (v. 41). Stephen is being accused of blasphemy of Moses, yet Israel's history is one of rejection of Moses (v. 39).

• verses 44 to 50 relate to blasphemy against God. Solomon built God's house (v. 47), and yet the idea of God being tied to a place is rejected (vv. 49,50; cf. Isa. 66:1–22), Solomon having said as much (2 Chr. 6:18 ff.).

Stephen makes it clear that God cannot be localized. He was with Abraham in Mesopotamia (v. 2), with Joseph in Egypt (v. 9), and with Moses at Mount Sinai (v. 30). He could not be limited to a calf, a tabernacle, or a temple – He is the pilgrim God.

As to blasphemy against Moses, the nation has always been guilty of that. As to blasphemy against God, Israel has not only localized God to the Temple but, at the same time, has rejected God's true Temple, the Lord Jesus, for it is in Him that God and people meet.

In verses 51 to 53, Stephen describes Israel's leaders with Gentile descriptions. They have always been consistent in rejecting God's messengers, despite the advantage of receiving God's law (v. 53). Here is a speech for the defence, but as in Peter and John's appearance before the Sanhedrin in chapter 4, Stephen is on the attack. It is his accusers who are being accused.

Why does Luke give so much space to the speech? Probably for two reasons. First, because of its place in the wider context; the death of Stephen will be the event which causes a major advance of the gospel to Gentile lands. Secondly, we see a model defence of pure Christianity in the face of Jewish antagonism.

REFLECTION

In what ways is the experience of Stephen, the church's first martyr, like that of Christ? Does God still deal with people the way He dealt with Israel in verses 39–43? Verse 42 says, God 'gave them over'. See Romans 1:24,26,28.

In Acts 2:37, we see deep conviction come upon those who have heard Peter's sermon. Stephen's speech also arouses a deep response (v. 54). Stephen pulls no punches (vv. 51,52). His manner and content is not that of a man looking for acquittal. Yet again we are told by Luke of his fullness in the Spirit in verse 55, as we were previously told in 6:5,8.

Stephen inflames the situation further by claiming to see the Son of Man standing at the right hand of God (v. 56). To the Jew, that any figure should be on equal footing with God was clearly blasphemous, for God is one. So, out of control with rage, they rush to stone him (vv. 57,58). Jesus had ascended to *stand* at God's right hand (Acts 2:34). Here He stands to welcome His first martyr into heaven.

Luke now introduces one of the main characters of his narrative, Saul. He will become better known by his Roman name, Paul (v. 58 and 8:1). Saul has clearly heard Stephen and, as the custodian of the cloaks of the witnesses against Stephen who will throw the first stones, he obviously approves of what is about to happen. Stephen is very much like the Lord Jesus in his death –'receive my spirit' (v. 59; cf. Luke 23:46), 'do not hold this sin against them' (v. 60;

cf. Luke 23:34). Was Stephen's prayer effective? In the case of Saul, it was.

The focus in the narrative now begins to shift, for God's gospel is on the move, from Jerusalem to Samaria, from Jew to semi-Jew and then to Gentile, from Jerusalem to Antioch, and from Peter to Paul. Change is a constant for the Christian. The gospel never changes, yet is always on the move, conquering lives wherever it goes. Even through the suffering and pain of its carriers, it continues on in triumph, as we shall see in chapter 8. God uses the death of Stephen to fling His messengers further out towards the ends of the earth. He is the sovereign God who will glorify Himself through our lives and even through our deaths.

REFLECTION

Why do you think the Jews of the Sanhedrin were so angry with Stephen? Why does the death of the apostle James, in Acts 12:2, get such a brief mention compared with the death of a deacon, Stephen, in Acts 7?

The early Christian Tertullian said, 'The blood of the martyrs is the seed of the church.'[4] The church scatters out from Jerusalem (Acts 11:19 ff.) and Saul initiates a thorough search for believers. There is nothing here of the open-mindedness of Gamaliel.

The body of Stephen was treated with respect and his loss was keenly felt (v. 2).

One of those who was scattered was Philip. He went to a city in Samaria. Through God's blessing, great joy came to the city. It is significant that Christian repentance is a turning from sin and a turning to God. In Thessalonica they turn away from the synagogue (Acts 17:1-9), in Athens from idols (Acts 17:34), and in Ephesus from superstitious sorcery (19:19). The 'turning from' may vary. Here, the people turn away from the flashy and spectacular emptiness offered by Simon and turn to the Lord Jesus and all that is involved in His kingdom (v. 12). The proclamation of Christ and His kingdom is what changes people.

Even Simon the sorcerer, astonished by what he saw, believed and was baptized (v. 13). (The Samaritans had an unusual experience of the Spirit, dealt with in tomorrow's reading.) Simon's motivation for believing, however, is apparently commercial. In verse 18 he offers to pay for the Holy Spirit. He is a reminder to us that not all who profess faith and are baptized are truly converted. A person can look good, have all the trappings, and still be 'full of bitterness and captive to sin' (v. 23). Simon's problem was that he understood neither the nature of Jesus' messiahship nor the person and role of the Holy Spirit. He thought of both as spiritual forces that could be used to gain control of people and make money, a common attitude of the world to 'the force' of Christianity.

God is about to authenticate true faith in the Samaritan believers (Acts 8:14–17), but at the same time Peter declares the truth about someone who is playing a game (Acts 8:20–23). Peter is exercising this ministry of authentication and exposure; he is exercising the ministry of keys (Matt. 16:17–20).

REFLECTION

How did Simon's unregenerate heart show itself? Do people still desire the Spirit, and how do they receive Him, according to Acts 19:1–6 and Acts 2:38,39?

Today's passage has been the source of much controversy in the church. Peter and John are sent by the apostles to Samaria, they lay hands on the disciples who have been baptized in Jesus' name (v. 16), and they receive the Holy Spirit (v. 17). Whose name should they have been baptized with in order to receive this Holy Spirit? It is clear they were true believers. Why had they not received the Holy Spirit at the time of their repentance, as did the 3,000 in Acts 2?

Some find here, in this two-stage experience, the basis for the practice of confirmation. That is, through the hand of the confirming bishop, the confirmee receives the Holy Spirit. Others argue that the normal Christian experience is two-stage; conversion is followed by Spirit baptism as a subsequent, second experience. Though other passages in Acts are cited to prove this point, the Acts 8 incident is the clearest.

Why was there a two-stage experience for the Samaritans when for the rest, God forgives our sin and gives us the Holy Spirit at one time (Acts 2:38,39)? Should Christians seek further full-ness of the Holy Spirit beyond their conversion, thinking that without this second blessing they have not received all God intended for them? If this is the case, why don't any of the New Testament letters urge the seeking of such a second blessing to solve any of the pastoral issues dealt with by the New Testament? Without backing from the letters of the New Testament for this belief in subsequence, was there a good historical reason for a two-stage blessing at Samaria?

There was ongoing conflict between Jews and Samaritans and such tension was not to be tolerated in the church. Therefore, Samaritan believers needed to realize that they were not a separate sect within Christianity, and so they received the Holy Spirit through the hands of the Jerusalem apostles. They were part of the one body of Christ. It was also important for Jerusalem believers to know that Samaritan believers were not inferior; the same Holy Spirit filled each. So Peter and John were eyewitnesses of the integrity of the Samaritan believers' experience.

There are so many characters, stories and experiences of salvation in Acts. It is not Luke's intention to show the normative spiritual experience for today.

REFLECTION

Simon sought commercial value from the Holy Spirit (vv. 18–24). Why is Peter's response appropriate? See Ephesians 1:13,14. What elements make up the normal Christian experience?

So far we have read of large numbers of people coming to repentance and faith in Jesus (see Acts 2:41,47; 4:4; 6:7). Now we meet just one man, who highlights God's interest in each and every person.

Philip is directed by the angel to the Jerusalem to Gaza road. He meets an Ethiopian on his way home from Jerusalem, reading the scrolls of Isaiah. The Spirit directs Philip to the chariot (v. 29) and Philip asks the Ethiopian if he understands what he is reading. The man invites Philip into the chariot and asks him to explain Isaiah 53:7,8 (vv. 31–33). Philip explains that Isaiah is referring to Jesus, and no doubt tells the man that he must repent and be baptized (Acts 2:38) as a public display of his repentance. The eunuch is baptized and Philip is taken away by the Spirit of the Lord (v. 39).

The great evangelist of Acts is God Himself. His angel gives Philip his direction. He prepares the Ethiopian, who just happens to be reading the great messianic passage of Isaiah 53. He appoints him to hear the message. He ordains his response (see Acts 11:18).

What might Philip's message have been? Look at Isaiah 53:5–12:

- our sin was laid to Christ's account – verse 5;

- we are all sinful people – verse 6;

- He voluntarily gave Himself for the sin of His people – verses 7 and 8;

- He will be vindicated and see the fruit of His work – verses 10 to 12.

The Ethiopian's response (v. 36) would indicate that Philip had called upon him to repent and be baptized. We ought not to be paralyzed by God's sovereignty in salvation. God directs, prepares and ordains, but He chooses to bring people to faith through human messengers – 'faith comes from hearing the message' (Rom. 10:17).

God is ever reaching out to people. He makes us 'fishers of men' (Matt. 4:19). He urges us to pray for labourers for the harvest field. He sends His Son to be Saviour and His Spirit to be co-witness. And He mandates us to explain the truth (v. 31).

REFLECTION

What caused such rejoicing to the Ethiopian (v. 39)? Reflect on the ministry of Philip in chapter 8. What ups and downs did he experience?

Here is a major turning point in Acts and in the history of the church. Luke repeats incidents in his narrative for emphasis (see Acts 22:6–21; 26:12–18).

Paul never forgets what a zealous persecutor of the church he was (Phil. 3:6, 1 Tim. 1:15,16; 1 Cor. 15:9). He had authority from the high priest in Jerusalem to arrest followers of the Way in the synagogues of Damascus, and take them back to Jerusalem. His experience is much like that of Moses in Exodus 3:2 ff.:

• a light, a voice (Acts 9:3,4; Exod. 3:2–4);

• the solemn repetition of the name 'Saul, Saul' (Acts 9:4) and 'Moses! Moses!' (Exod 3:4).

Notice Jesus asks Saul why Saul is persecuting Him (v. 4). Jesus takes persecution of the followers of the Way personally; to persecute them is to persecute Him. One of Saul's first lessons is to learn of the solidarity of the believer and Christ. It is little wonder that the concept of being 'in Christ' dominates His teaching (see Matt. 10:40). Jesus' question indicates that He is looking for the reason for Saul's zealous persecution. Saul, however, is far more interested in who is addressing Him (v. 5). Jesus identifies Himself by His earthly name and address (v. 5; Acts 22:8) as the one who in reality is being persecuted by Saul. The Lord Jesus, however, has plans for Saul, and tells him to go into Damascus and wait (v. 6).

Saul understands the Damascus road experience as his conversion, his seeing of the resurrected Christ (1 Cor. 9:1; 15:8). The conversion of such a zealous persecutor as Saul provides further evidence for the truth and power of the gospel to save. No one could argue that Saul's seeing the resurrected Christ was wishful thinking on his part.

The zealous persecutor becomes the zealous apostle. 'Amazing grace! (how sweet the sound) That sav'd a wretch like me!'[5]

REFLECTION

What are some of the characteristics evidenced by Jesus on the Damascus road? Why do you think the conversion of Saul is such a major turning point for Luke?

Ananias is rightfully cautious about his vision (v. 10). The Lord is specific about the direction He gives (v. 11). He has wonderfully prepared the way for Ananias (v. 12).

Ananias knows all about Saul. He does not want to go anywhere near him (vv. 13,14). The Lord is insistent (v. 15). Saul's commissioning as the apostle to the Gentiles is repeated by Saul in each of the accounts of his conversion (22:21; 26:17). It is clear that his Gentile focus is not exclusive as he begins preaching the divinity of Jesus in the Damascus synagogues (v. 21). Whereas Peter had to have a special vision to be convinced of God's purpose to include the Gentiles in His people (10:9 to 11:18), there was no such hesitation for Paul. He was a stubborn resister of Christ but, once that resistance was broken, he realized that the gospel was for all.

Along with his partners, he takes the gospel throughout Asia and into Europe, to the synagogues first and then to the fields, the marketplaces and the lecture halls. He does not hesitate to make clear that Yahweh is no local deity whose promises are for Jews only. Jesus is universal Lord, Judgement Day is coming and all people should repent in preparation (Acts 17:30,31). What an effect it all has on the hearers!

Campbell Morgan, in his commentary on Acts, puts it this way:

> Look at Europe today in spite of all its desolation. Think of her architecture, then blot out the temples erected to the worship of Christ and what remains? Go into her picture galleries and destroy the paintings inspired by the Christian faith and what will be left? Go into her halls of music, examine her literature, then destroy all that has been made possible and inspired by the Christian movement, and what will abide? ... Essentially the measure of Europe's freedom is the measure in which she has obeyed the principles of Christianity. The measure of her purity is the measure in which she has obeyed the word to the gaoler, 'Believe in the Lord Jesus and you will be saved.' (Acts 16:31)[6]

REFLECTION

Think about the model of discipleship provided to us by Ananias. How much of what is good about our culture is the fruit of the Christian gospel?

Adam and Eve wanted paradise but they did not want God. Does our society do the same – wanting the fruit of the faith without the faith?

Saul baffled the Jews in Damascus who expected him to defend Judaism against the new movement, but now he is preaching that Jesus is the Son of God (v. 20) and that Jesus is the Christ (v. 22). Luke tells of their reaction; they are astonished (v. 21) and baffled (v. 22). Meanwhile, Saul grows more and more powerful. He cannot be beaten in argument, and so the Jews plan to kill him (v. 23). Here is another example of unreasonable and unreasoning blind belligerence.

The reluctance of the brethren in Jerusalem to accept Saul is only broken by the encouraging intervention of Barnabas (v. 27). Saul's activities are described as bold speech (v. 28), and talk and debate (v. 29), but again the last resort is not to recognize his argument but to seek to kill him (v. 29). For his own safety he is sent to his hometown of Tarsus.

The following verse (v. 31) is a summary of the life of the church at this time. It is probably about AD. 35. The church now has a time of peace. It is free of external threat, strengthened and encouraged by the Holy Spirit, growing numerically and living in reverence for God. With Saul's conversion, the persecutions which followed the death of Stephen come to an end.

Luke's description of Saul's conversion is now complete. He was indeed God's chosen instrument to bring about the spread of the gospel throughout the Roman Empire. F.F. Bruce says Paul's contribution to the Gentile mission was 'unique and far reaching'. He summarizes his emphases:

- true religion is not a matter of rules but an expression of the indwelling Spirit in love;
- in Christ, people constitute the new humanity;
- people matter more than things, principles more than causes;
- discrimination on the basis of race, religion, class or sex is an offence against God and humanity alike.

'If these lessons are important, it is well to give grateful credit to one man who taught them.'[7]

REFLECTION

Note the experience of the church in Acts 9:31 compared with 6:7. Why will the church described in 9:31 always be blessed with growth? Saul's opposition to Christ is apparent from chapters 7 – 9. How is his union with Christ now shown in 9:20–30? How is your union with Christ evident?

DAY 25

READ Acts 9:32–43

The book of Acts has had many names throughout its life – for example 'The Deeds of the Apostles', 'The Acts of All the Apostles', 'The Acts of the Holy Spirit' and 'What Jesus Continued To Do'. Some of these titles seek to express the truth that in the gospel is the record of what Jesus did in His life on earth, while in Acts we have the record of what Jesus continues to do through His Spirit, as He sits at God's right hand.

The account of Peter's raising Dorcas is very similar to the account in Luke 8:49–56 of the raising of Jairus's daughter. There is no doubt that the girl and the woman are dead – the professional mourners for Jairus' daughter have arrived (Luke 8:52) and Dorcas's body has been washed ready for burial (Acts 9:37). Peter had been with Jesus at the resurrection of Jairus's daughter and he is so bold as to pray that Jesus would do it again in the case of Dorcas.

A creation miracle is required for resurrection to take place. The brain would have to return to life, for it has been denied oxygen. But the fact that so many trust in the Lord as a result of Dorcas's resurrection (v. 42) underlines its reality. Why do we find it so hard to believe in resurrection? Jesus is Lord of

life and death. He has defeated death and He exercises rule over it as He sees fit.

Blaise Pascal put it like this:

Atheists: What reason have they for saying that we cannot rise from the dead? Which is more difficult; to be born, or to be raised from the dead, for what has never been to exist, or for what has been to exist again? Is it more difficult to come into being than to return to it? Custom makes the one seem easy, while unfamiliarity makes the other impossible. But that is a popular way of judging![8]

REFLECTION

In what ways does Dorcas model Christian character for us? Acts 9:32–43 is a description of a vital church life. What qualities described can we pray that God would duplicate in His church today? What has been the most encouraging aspect of these studies in Acts 1 – 9 for you?

29

Again Luke reminds us that God is the sovereign and active evangelist. He is the expansive God, dealing with a people of limited vision. In this case Peter, the foremost apostle to the Jews.

Peter's understanding of Jesus' words in Luke 24:47 has remained limited. At the beginning of Acts 10, he believes God's intention is to bring the gospel not to peoples of all nations, but to the Jews of all nations.

God firstly prepares the Gentile, Cornelius (vv. 1–8). He is a devout, well-respected, God-fearing centurion who identifies with the synagogue and yet is uncircumcised. Though a God-fearer, he is still technically an unclean Gentile. Despite his morality and generosity, he is still in need of Christian conversion.

Luke reminds us that Peter was staying in the house of a tanner (see Acts 9:43; 10:6; 10:32). This occupation was considered unclean.

Having prepared Cornelius, God now prepares Peter (vv. 9–23). He is given a vision of clean and unclean food and told to eat it. Peter replies, 'Surely not, Lord!' He has never eaten unclean food.

The lesson for Peter is that the distinction between clean and unclean no longer applies to food or to people (v. 15). This is what Jesus implied when He taught that it is not what enters a man from outside that makes him unclean, but what comes from within (see Mark 7:17–23). God is preparing Peter to leap an enormous barrier in his thinking. Just at the moment he is reflecting on the vision (v. 17), Peter is told that messengers from Cornelius have arrived and that he is to go with them.

God's purpose is not only that Jews, but also non-Jews should hear the gospel and be saved. Peter needed to learn that old distinctions about what or with whom you eat no longer apply.

REFLECTION

Do we believe that people need to earn the right to receive the gospel? How might this reflect itself in our evangelism? As fine a man as Cornelius was, he nevertheless needed the peace that comes through Jesus Christ. Are there people you are tempted to believe may not need to hear the gospel?

The God of the intersection laid down in eternity is about to bring Peter and Cornelius together in a groundbreaking, evangelistic encounter.

Peter, the opportunistic evangelist of earlier chapters, seems quite blind to the opportunity he has of preaching to Cornelius and his friends. Here he is a reluctant evangelist (vv. 28,29). He still hasn't realized that God's saving purposes could include non-Jews.

When Cornelius tells Peter about God's dealings with him, the 'penny finally drops' (v. 34). Peter preaches a three-point sermon that closely follows the overall structure of Mark's Gospel (Peter was the primary source of Mark's Gospel).

1. The exemplary life of Jesus (vv. 37,38).

2. The death and resurrection of Jesus, which Peter witnessed (vv. 39–41).

3. The coming judgement by Jesus, and that forgiveness of sin is available through Him (vv. 42,43).

In Acts 2, the Holy Spirit comes before the preaching, and in Acts 8, after the preaching. Here in Acts 10, he comes during the preaching, before Peter reaches the call to repent. God takes control of this evangelistic encounter.

In verse 45, the witnesses to this event are called 'circumcised believers'. The critical point is that the Holy Spirit has fallen on the uncircumcised, without them meeting the prerequisite of baptism or circumcision. The distinction between clean and unclean people has been removed. Peter stays on with the new Gentile believers for a few days (v. 48). No doubt they ate together. We are not told what was on the menu, but in God's eyes it was all clean, just as all those present were clean, because of the peace that comes through Jesus Christ (v. 36).

REFLECTION

God is directing Peter to 'press beyond the fringe' in his evangelistic concerns. In what ways does this section encourage you to reach out?

What does this episode tell you about God? (See 1 Tim. 2:3,4.)

News travels quickly. The news of the Holy Spirit's coming on the Gentiles reaches Jerusalem before Peter does. The church there is horrified by reports of Peter mixing with Gentiles (v. 3). Peter vividly describes what happened at Cornelius's house, noting that he had six witnesses with him when he went there (v. 12).

Earlier in Acts, Peter asks the Sanhedrin to judge if it is right to obey them or to obey God (4:19). Here, as he tells his Christian brothers in Jerusalem about the events at Cornelius's house, he applies the same principle. Peter wasn't about to oppose God by denying water baptism to those whom God had baptized in the Spirit (v. 17).

All objections are dropped (v. 18) and the Jerusalem church praises God that He has given the gift of repentance to non-Jews.

This is an important turning point in the church's life. Luke indicates its importance by reporting it three times (see Acts 10; 11; 15:1–11). Luke again shows us people 'warts and all'. Tanning was considered an unclean activity, and although Luke tells us Peter was staying at Simon the tanner's house, Peter makes no mention of this in his report to his Jewish brothers (v. 11:5). We see that Peter is human after all. He was happy to accept hospitality from an unclean Jew, but to do so from an unclean Gentile was unthinkable. It required a vision from God to arrest his prejudice. This is a stark reminder that the best of men are men, at best.

REFLECTION

How does the description of the Gentile experience in 11:18 help us in our evangelistic efforts? Are there people who we have categorized as 'off-limits' to the gospel? If so, how must our attitudes change in light of Acts 10 – 11?

The church at Antioch, north of Jerusalem, is the mother of all Gentile Christian churches. Due to God's work (v. 21), there was a great number of believers there, and so the Jerusalem church responds by appointing Barnabas and sending him as their representative to nurture the work.

When Barnabas arrives in Antioch, an even greater number of people are added to the church (v. 24). Luke reports that Barnabas brought with him Saul from Tarsus. Then, for a third time, he tells of great numbers of people in Antioch (v. 26).

Barnabas was an encourager (v. 23). Both he and Saul established the church by providing sound teaching for a whole year (v. 26). At Antioch, believers are first called Christians, literally, 'people of the anointing' (v. 26).

Luke describes a well-taught church, showing clear evidence of repentance and faith. The church at Antioch

- listens to and respects the prophetic word of Agabus (v. 28);

- responds to the Word with financial generosity (v. 29);

- is culturally diverse. This is reflected in their leaders, who include Jews, a black African and a north African (13:1–3);

- has leaders who are sensitive to the voice of the Holy Spirit (13:2);

- generously shares their finances and their personnel (13:3).

This presents a great challenge to the mindset that would keep the best for self and let God have the rest.

Again, the expansive purpose of God is at the forefront of events. Luke records that the Holy Spirit said, 'Set apart for me Barnabas and Saul for the work to which I have called them' (13:2). Other similar words of God are recorded in Acts 5:20; 8:26, 9:15; 10:20; 16:9 and 18:10.

REFLECTION

Do I keep the best and share the rest? Does my church see its role as establishing people well in God's grace and then acting as a clearing house, sending people out and seeing them move beyond the fringe?

 **DAY 30** **READ** Acts 12

Here is evidence of God's hidden hand at work. Chapter 12 begins so well for Herod. James is decapitated and Peter is imprisoned. Yet, the chapter ends with Herod being struck down, eaten by worms and dying (v. 23). The turning point is verse 5, where we are told the church earnestly prayed to God for Peter. Luke contrasts Herod's political authority with God's sovereign control. Peter is very well guarded in prison, but the angel of God delivers him (vv. 6–10). The callous Herod has the soldiers who had been assigned to guard Peter executed (v. 19).

Luke could have omitted verses 12 to 17, but he doesn't. He deliberately shows the church's unbelief in its own prayers. Their prayer is effective, but imperfect. Their prayer is answered, but the pray-ers themselves find it unbelievable. When we are tempted to have faith in our own prayers, or to think that prayer is somehow forcing the hand of a reluctant God, here we see that God is greater than our praying. Here, He graciously answers unbelieving prayer.

During the course of his quarrel with the people of Tyre and Sidon, Herod had cut off their food supplies. Why else would they respond as they did to his speech in verse 22? Then, Herod is struck down. It is ironic that the one who denied food to Tyre becomes food for worms.

Peter is delivered, Herod is dead and Luke tells us that the Word of God is healthy indeed (v. 24). This is an encouraging start to the Gentile mission (v. 25). These radical reversals are evidence that the progress of the gospel is unstoppable.

REFLECTION

In what ways are you encouraged by the vitality of the Word of God and its messengers, in contrast to Herod's wormy death? Dark days come to all of us. How does this chapter provide reassurance in the midst of darkness?

Acts is great literature. Great literature has many layers of subtle meaning, and Acts is no exception.

In chapter 13, the first missionary journey begins. Note how Luke uses the names of people and places to provide emphasis, irony, comparison and contrast.

Barnabas and Saul are sent on their way (v. 2). Note that Barnabas is listed before Saul in this verse. This becomes significant as we read of their progress in subsequent chapters (see Reflection below).

Their first stop is Cyprus, Barnabas' home (see Acts 4:36). As they travel, they move from east to west and, even though the Gentile church has commissioned them, they begin by preaching in the synagogue at each town (v. 5).

In Paphos they meet a Jewish sorcerer, Bar-Jesus (v. 6), a name that literally means 'son of Jesus'. This man acts as an advisor to the Roman representative, Sergius Paulus. In verse 8, Luke uses the sorcerer's Greek name, Elymas, subtly highlighting his heretical character. This man is a Jew using a Greek name.

Saul recognizes the sorcerer's true character. He is not a 'son of Jesus', but a 'child of the devil' (v. 10). The man is struck with blindness. This is the first sign, or miracle, God performs through Saul, and it is a declaration of judgement, very much like Saul's own experience (Acts 9:8,9). Sergius is an intelligent man and, upon seeing what happened to his advisor and, having heard the word of God, he believes (v. 12).

From this point on in Acts, Luke uses Saul's Greek name, Paul, and this is another example of his subtle use of names to convey meaning. In the wider context of Acts, Paul is a more fitting name for the apostle, given that his ministry extended across an empire in which Greek was the common language.

In chapter 13, Luke uses the name change to indicate a close connection between the senate's representative, Sergius Paulus, and God's representative, Paul. Perhaps his intention is to show that Paul is on equal footing with these Roman provincial leaders.

REFLECTION

Why do you think Luke shows such interest in names? Look at Acts 4:36, 11:26, 13:6,8–10. Why do you think the order in which names is used is significant? See Acts 13:2; 13:46; 14:1; 15:2; 15:12.

The missionary party, now minus John Mark, moves on to Pisidian Antioch and visits the synagogue there.

Paul is now clearly the spokesman (v. 16) and his name precedes Barnabas's in verses 46 and 50. There is no evidence of competition. The order simply reflects the reality of giftedness and leadership. This reminds us of the old saying, 'It takes more grace than I can tell, to play the second fiddle well.'

Paul now speaks like Stephen as he reviews the history of God's people, Israel. Here, he makes the only reference to his namesake, King Saul, in the New Testament (vv. 21,22). Saul's reign is remembered for its lack of regard for God's word.

Paul says that God has sent the Son of David, the Saviour, Jesus, and that through Jesus salvation is now available for Jews and God-fearing Gentiles (vv. 16–26). This Jesus was rejected by His own people, killed, raised from the dead by God, and seen by many witnesses (vv. 27–31).

The Sanhedrin had not allowed Stephen to get this far through his sermon (see Acts 7), and Paul makes the most of this opportunity to emphasize the resurrection of Jesus is the fulfilment of Psalm 2 (vv. 32–37).

You would expect Paul, as the author of Romans and Galatians, to speak as he does in verses 38 and 39. The law cannot save (vv. 32,33,39). It is by faith in this man Jesus, rather than observance of the law, that salvation (vv. 23,26), good news (v. 32) and forgiveness of sin (vv. 38,39) have come.

There is a strong note of warning (v. 41), but some did find salvation as they heard God's word preached by Paul that day (vv. 42,43).

The next week, there is a massive turnout to hear the word. The Jews, motivated by jealousy, oppose the gospel, and so Paul and Barnabas turn their attention to the preaching to the Gentiles (v. 46).

In a typical summary statement, Luke reports in verses 48–52:

- the wider spread of the gospel;

- opposition from the Jews;

- the shaking of dust off the feet, and

- fullness of joy and the Holy Spirit in the believers.

REFLECTION

Note how Luke emphasizes this is God's work (v. 48). How are you encouraged as you see God fulfilling His work? Do you see yourself as God's co-worker, bearing an unstoppable message?

The first missionary journey continues with visits to Iconium (vv. 1–7), Lystra and Derbe (vv. 8–20). The visit to Iconium features bold proclamation of the gospel, signs and wonders. At Lystra, Paul's first miracle of healing takes place (vv. 8–10).

There are striking parallels in Luke's description of the public emergence of Jesus and Paul:

- Luke 4:1–13: Jesus confronts the devil;
  Acts 13:4–12: Paul confronts the child of the devil.
- Luke 4:14–30: Jesus preaches in the synagogue and is rejected;
  Acts 13:13–43: Paul preaches in the synagogue to a divided response.
- Luke 4:38–44; 5:17–26: Jesus heals many, including a paralytic;
  Acts 14:8–10: Paul heals a paralytic.

Just as Jesus the Saviour emerges into the public arena, so does His primary representative in the Gentile world. Paul is in solidarity with Jesus, and Jesus continues His work through Paul.

There is also a parallel here with Peter's healing of the paralytic (Acts 3). This demonstrates Paul's apostleship is of the same order as Peter's.

The people of Lystra want to give Paul and Barnabas divine status. Their response (vv. 14,15) is a clear contrast to Herod's in chapter 12.

Paul responds to these people with a clear message to a pagan audience, whose lives are dominated by agricultural cycles (vv. 15–17). Firstly, he insists on the humanness of the messenger. Secondly, that God the creator has shown kindness by giving rain, crops, food and joy. Thirdly, people should turn from the worship of men to the living God. Finally, God's attitude to humanity has been patient acceptance, but that has now changed (see Acts 17:30).

The pattern of this message is very close to Paul's description of the conversion of the Thessalonians (see 1 Thess. 1:9,10).

Once more the Jews win the crowd and, consequently, Paul is stoned and left for dead. Later, the team returns and encourages the believers by telling them what is in store for them (v. 22).

We must not be unrealistic as we face the future. Unrealistic expectations always cause doubt. See how Jesus tells the disciples what is ahead of them in John 16:1,4,33. Such warnings are given to us for the same reason as to the first Christians in Lystra – to strengthen and encourage them (and us) 'to remain true to the faith' (v. 22).

REFLECTION

Prosperity theology is often popular, teaching that following Jesus leads to health and wealth. How does what you are reading in Acts challenge this thinking and teaching? Opposition to the gospel is inevitable. What response is called for in the face of such opposition?

This section has been called the centerpiece, the watershed, the turning point of the book of Acts.

This meeting of the church at Jerusalem is framed by Paul's first and second missionary journeys. The purpose of this first church council is to consider the nature of the true gospel. The matter of concern is that some Jewish believers were urging Gentile believers to be circumcised, in order to be saved (vv. 1–5). This is the same concern addressed by Paul in his letter to the Galatians. He wrote this letter during his stay at Antioch (see Acts 14:28). If the church embraced this teaching, Christianity would become a mere sect of Judaism.

Such additions to the gospel, even if thought to be good and helpful things such as sacramental observance, are dangerous. They take our focus away from the sufficiency of Christ's work alone as the means by which we are set right with God.

The debate is recorded in verses 6 to 12. This is Peter's last appearance in Acts, and he clearly states his conviction (v.11). Barnabas and Paul underline God's accreditation of their ministry (v. 12).

James, the Lord's brother and leader of the Jerusalem church, diplomatically refers to Peter by his Hebrew name, Simeon (v. 14), but quotes Amos 9:11–14 from the Greek translation of the Old Testament. In doing so, he recognizes the presence of a number of Greek-speakers. He says:

- the restored kingdom of God will include Gentiles (vv. 16,17);

- the people of God will include Gentiles (v. 14).

On the basis of what God has done and said, it is concluded there will be no additions to the true gospel. In verses 19 to 21, we read that a letter is drawn up and the decision is circulated.

Things that go without saying need to be said! Salvation is by grace alone, through faith alone, in Christ alone. There must be no additions or subtractions to the true gospel.

This very minute, a sinner who is not circumcised, baptized or confirmed may come to Jesus and, by repentance and faith, receive freely, immediately and forever, the forgiveness of sin, the gift of the Holy Spirit and a warm reception into God's worldwide family.

REFLECTION

Think about some of the things you add, or are tempted to add, to the gospel, as a supplement to the work of Christ. By adding these things, have your standards of acceptance of other professing Christians become higher than those of God?

The important letter from the church council at Jerusalem is circulated via Judas and Silas.

The inclusion of sexual immorality (v. 29) amongst the four things the recipients will do well to avoid is unusual. Surely the other matters – eating food offered to idols, blood, and the meat of strangled animals – are matters of liberty, which can be avoided for the sake of fellowship with Jewish believers, to whom these would be matters of sensitivity. Sexual immorality however, is not a matter of liberty. Why is it listed here?

All four are activities associated with pagan temples. Therefore, they are no longer appropriate behaviour for believers. Here, the general word used for sexual immorality (Greek, *porneia*) is best understood to refer to ritual temple prostitution. Therefore, the message is that Gentiles are to turn from idolatry and all pagan temple activities, including prostitution.

Two ironic events follow, in a chapter that does so much to ensure unity amongst believers.

Firstly, verses 36 to 41 tell of the disagreement between Paul and Barnabas over John Mark's leaving the first missionary journey (see Acts 13:13).

This is a sad event, and yet it leads to good, with two missionary teams being formed to advance the work of the gospel.

Secondly, in 16:1–5 we read of Paul's ironic request for the uncircumcised Timothy to be circumcised, so that the Jews will listen to his preaching. Paul resists circumcision when it is imposed as a necessity for salvation. However, when there is no such demand and it serves to facilitate the gospel's acceptance, Paul has Timothy circumcised. After all, it is a neutral surgical act.

John Newton, the eighteenth-century pastor and hymn writer, said of Paul, he 'was a reed in non-essentials – an iron pillar in essentials.'[9]

The next time you think of 'timid Timothy', remember his ready submission in this matter at about the age of 20.

REFLECTION

What do these verses teach us about Paul, Barnabas and Timothy and their priorities? Why is 16:5 such an appropriate conclusion to this section?

Until now, the gospel has advanced in Gentile territory through rural Asia, the region we know as modern-day Turkey. People have been won over, but some critics might claim they were just gullible, simple folk. Now the missionaries come to Europe (Macedonia) and its prosperous commercial and intellectual cities.

Under the oversight of God, Paul has a vision of a man from Europe (v. 9) calling him to come and help. This was the call of God for work to begin in Europe, and the first city Paul and his team visits is Philippi.

In the absence of a synagogue in the city, they know they will find Jews and God-fearers meeting by the river. They find just such a group, and Lydia becomes the first European convert – God is active here (v. 14). Lydia is baptized and extends hospitality to the missionaries.

The conversion of the fortune-telling slave girl (vv. 16–18) and her spiritual insight (v. 17) leads to the first opposition in Europe, and it arises for commercial reasons (v. 19).

Paul and Silas are flogged and imprisoned. Surely the gospel has come to a dead end. But no – there is an earthquake, the chains of all the prisoners are loosened, but none of them escape.

The fortune-teller earlier said, 'These men ... are telling you the way to be saved.' Now, the jailer asks, 'what must I do to be saved?' (v. 30). He is told he will be saved if he believes in the Lord Jesus Christ (v. 31).

This callous man who had beaten and flogged Paul and Silas, now bathes the wounds he had inflicted (v. 33). He and his family are baptized and 'set a meal before them' (v. 34). What a remarkable day for that household.

The first church at Philippi (v. 40) was very diverse – a woman of wealth with a household, a slave girl, the cruel jailer and his household now transformed, and some others. Jew and Greek, slave and free, male and female – all one in Christ Jesus (see also Gal. 3:28).

After upholding their legal rights as Roman citizens, Paul and Silas are asked to leave the city, and they do so, in their own time.

Paul has been stoned at Lystra and left for dead. Now he has been stripped, beaten, severely flogged and imprisoned. Beware of too quickly glossing over the agonizing pain involved in these experiences.

REFLECTION

What do you learn from the experiences of Paul and his fellow missionaries? What does this teach you about perseverance in the face of adversity?

The gospel now comes to the seaport of Thessalonica. Ancient seaports were infamous for their prosperity and licentiousness.

Here, the Jewish opposition seems to have been especially tough and persistent (v. 13). The immorality of the city probably contributed to the toughness of these Jews – they had to be strong in order to maintain their separateness from the local community.

For three weeks, Paul reasoned, explained and proved (vv. 2,3) the gospel – the suffering, death and resurrection of Jesus, the Messiah.

It is important to note that in this especially difficult environment, it is the same gospel that is powerful. Martyn Lloyd-Jones, after conducting a university mission in Oxford in 1941, said, 'There is no greater fallacy than to think that you need a gospel for special types of people.'[10]

Jewish opposition is driven by jealousy (v. 5), though the reason they cite is loyalty to Caesar (v. 7). This is just like the opponents in Philippi who used concern for community as a cover for greed (Acts 16:20,21). In the King James Version of the Bible, verse 5 reads, the Jews gathered 'certain lewd fellows of the baser sort' to cause uproar in the city.

The Bereans, forty miles away, nobly examine the Scriptures in the light of the gospel. They were eager to hear, and many came to believe (vv. 11,12).

The Jews from Thessalonica pursue the missionaries and oppose them in Berea before Paul leaves and is escorted to Athens.

In each of the five cities visited on this second missionary journey – Philippi, Thessalonica, Berea, Athens and Corinth – there is gospel preaching, a response of faith from some, and opposition from others. God is sovereign. His purpose is not thwarted. He uses the bad reception as much as the glad reception to see His purposes fulfilled.

REFLECTION

To be forewarned is to be forearmed. We should not be surprised when we encounter opposition to the gospel. Why are we so taken aback by opposition to gospel work? The Bereans were of noble character (v. 11). Note the reason they are described this way. What do you learn from their example?

The gospel now comes to Athens, the centre of intellectual and philosophical speculation in the ancient world. Paul is distressed to find the city full of idols (v. 16). The scholarly Luke shows his frustration at the 'airy fairy' nature of the Athenians (v. 21).

Paul uses as his point of contact with the people the altar 'To An Unknown God' (v. 23), and he reasons with the Athenians:

• you do not create a place for God to live – a temple. Rather, He has created a place for you to live (v. 24,26);

• God is not dependent on us. We are dependent on Him (v. 25);

• God is not lost. We are. He has taken the first step towards us (vv. 26–28);

• we are God's offspring. He is not our offspring (v. 29).

At every point the Athenians minimized God and maximized themselves.

Paul preaches true wisdom; such wisdom is harmonizing with reality (v. 31) – the reality is that God has fixed the Day of Judgement. The proof of this is that He raised the judge from the dead. The resurrection of the judge proves that death was not the end for Him, and it will not be the end for us.

For there to be true harmony with this reality (v. 30), people must repent. They must end self-rule and recognize the rule of the one, true God.

Again, we read of the typical, divided response (vv. 32–34) – some sneered, others made further enquiry and, for Dionysius and Damaris and others, it was a never-to-be-forgotten day of repentance and new life.

To be a Christian is to lose control of your life to Jesus. Such was the experience of these repentant Athenians.

REFLECTION

Athens was a place of knowledge and intellectual stimulation. Yet, here Paul finds ignorance of the grossest kind. What do you find especially confronting about Paul's discovery? Can you think of contemporary parallels where places of knowledge become citadels of gross ignorance?

The gospel is 'boxing above its weight'. So far, it has won converts in four European cities, but now it comes to Corinth, the toughest of them all.

Corinth was located between two harbours and was renowned as a place of prosperity and wickedness.

Again, the Jews oppose Paul (v. 13). In response, Paul shakes the dust off his feet as a sign of God's judgement on their hardness of heart (v. 6). The missionaries leave the synagogue, and yet the gospel is still effective (vv. 7,8).

In each city where there is opposition, the opposition is used by God to open up new areas of endeavour. The missionaries left Philippi, came to Thessalonica, were sent to Berea, escorted to Athens, and then went out of the synagogue in Corinth into the house of Titius Justus (v. 7). God uses the bad as well as the glad to see His purposes fulfilled.

What keeps the missionaries going in the face of such opposition? Paul was not a loner – he had meaningful and supportive friendships (vv. 1–4). Paul was sustained by the timely arrival of Silas and Timothy and the good news they brought with them (v. 5; see also 1 Thess. 3:6). A direct word comes to Paul from God (vv. 9,10) – he is not to be anxious or silent, for God has His elect and will call them out through Paul's ministry.

Ministry is always a battle, but there will be a Lydia, a jailer, a Dionysius, Damaris, Jason (see Acts 17:5–9) and many others to encourage us along the way. God's message is unstoppable. He buries His messengers, never His message.

Paul's ministry was persuasive (Acts 17:4; 18:4) and he keeps persuading, right to the end (Acts 28:23,24). The fact of God's sovereign control in the face of fierce opposition means that Paul never backs off in his ministry. Even in his trial before Festus and King Agrippa, Agrippa says to Paul, 'Do you think that in such a short time you can persuade me to be a Christian?' (Acts 26:28).

Paul persuades as long as he has breath.

REFLECTION

What special promise of God encouraged Paul (vv. 9,10)? How does this word encourage you? Identify how each hindrance of the gospel recorded in these chapters opens up new opportunities for ministry. What does this teach you about God?

This brief report on the ministry at Ephesus follows Paul's initial contact there in Acts 18:19. It is sandwiched between two accounts of deficiency – those deficient because of ignorance, the disciples of John (19:1–7) and those who were deceitfully deficient, the seven sons of Sceva (19:13–16).

Paul does not tell the former group about the Spirit, but about Jesus (vv. 4,5). The latter group wants to 'use' the power of the Spirit, apart from relationship with Jesus.

The devil is not fooled. He is the master of fakery. His superior power stands in contrast to their powerless, superstitious spirituality.

The resultant burning of the magic scrolls, out of fear of God, and the contrasting health of the Word of the Lord provide a further, rich distinction (vv. 18–20).

Paul's church planting activities at Ephesus follow a familiar pattern (vv. 8–12). He begins at the synagogue, focusing persuasively on the kingdom of God. Then there arises Jewish opposition. Paul moves elsewhere to teach, proclaiming 'the word of the Lord' and God does 'extraordinary miracles' through him.

The Gentile antagonism at Ephesus is both commercially and theologically driven. Paul's insistence that 'man-made gods are no gods at all' (v. 26) is bad news for the sellers of silver shrines of Artemis. But, Demetrius is also concerned that the goddess will be 'robbed of her divine majesty' (v. 27). The irony is that of all people, it would be hardest for the silversmiths themselves to believe that they were making gods with their own hands.

The resultant outcry from the crowd gathered in the theatre, thought to hold 24,000 people, leads Luke to record two interesting events. Alexander (v. 33) is pushed forward by the Jews, but we will never know what he was going to say because he is drowned out by the crowd. The city clerk calms everyone down by reminding them of the proper legal channels for action against Paul (vv. 35–41).

REFLECTION

The seven sons of Sceva, like Ananias and Sapphira before them (Acts 5), are playing a part. Note how they and the evil spirit refer to Jesus in verses 13 and 15. Compare this with how Luke refers to Jesus in verses 13 and 17.

Who is fooled? How are they exposed? What results follow?

Of all the ministries in Acts, only one is reviewed – that at Ephesus. What Paul did at Ephesus is recorded in Acts 19:8–12. His review of what he did is given in today's reading.

Paul calls together the elders of the church at Ephesus to remind them of what they already know. He tells them what he did whilst he was with them, so that they can continue in like manner.

Paul's ministry was Word-based. He speaks of preaching and proclaiming (vv. 20,27), teaching (v. 20), declaring, testifying (vv. 21,24) and preaching (v. 25).

The content of his ministry is 'anything ... helpful', 'the gospel of God's grace', 'the kingdom' and 'the whole will of God'. The goal of this work is to encourage all people to 'turn to God in repentance and have faith in our Lord Jesus' (v. 21).

In verses 26 to 28, Paul uses two pictures to describe his ministry. They are:

• the watchman, who sounds a warning and is therefore innocent of the blood of those who fail to heed it;

• the shepherd, who must watch himself if he is to effectively guard others.

C.H. Spurgeon said in his lectures to his students, 'we shall be likely to accomplish most when we are in the best spiritual condition'.[11] According to Augustine, this type of self-watch consisted of 'praying, reading the word and weeping'.[12]

Remember, these verses are Paul's 'upper room discourse', his last word to his elders. The elders are to be diligent overseers, with ultimate confidence in God and His word of grace (v. 32), for ultimately, the flock is His, bought by Him, and is under His protection.

In the twenty-first-century world, that which is weighty is often trivialized, and that which is trivial, exalted. We must never allow the ministry of shepherding to be trivialized.

REFLECTION

Think about Paul's apostolic model of shepherding. Think about each element of this ministry – the Word; personal integrity; accountability. Think about the church in Ephesus – its beginning, recorded here; what it was like a little later, when Paul wrote his letter, and a generation later, when another letter arrives (see Rev. 2:1–7).

Paul has a conviction that he must go to Jerusalem, and after that, to Rome (Acts 19:21). He is both compelled and warned by the Spirit (Acts 20:22,23). Both danger and rescue are going to be Paul's experience.

His friends warn him not to go. Agabus warns him (vv. 10,11), and his fellow travellers plead with him not to go (v. 12), but he persists, insisting he is ready to die 'for the name of the Lord Jesus' (v. 13).

Just as it was for the Lord Jesus (Luke 18:31–33), Jerusalem will once more show itself to be a centre of aggressive opposition to the interests of the gospel.

We read that thousands of Jews have believed, but retain their zeal for the law (v. 20) and rumours abound that Paul disregards the Old Testament law (v. 21). Anticipating trouble, James urges Paul to join the purification rites of four men. As is evidenced in the case of Timothy's circumcision (16:3), Paul's attitude to the law was probably flexible, in cases where no gospel issue was involved. It may have been the outworking of 1 Corinthians 9:19,20.

Professor Blaiklock comments on these events: 'He sought to love, to understand, to act in selfless humility. The result, by that tragic irony which Heaven sometimes permits, was apparent disaster.'[13]

There is a riot. Wisely, the Romans had placed their barracks near the Temple, and the garrison is on hand to rescue Paul from his own people. This rescue is the first of four. (The others are recorded in Acts 22:24; 23:10; 23:20 and 23:31.)

Paul is thus rescued from a hopeless situation, four times. Each time rescue comes from an unlikely quarter. The original word spoken to Ananias in Acts 9:15 to 16 is being fulfilled.

God can be trusted to exercise careful oversight of His church as it seeks to promote the gospel in the world.

REFLECTION

Paul earlier listens to Agabus (11:27–30). Why doesn't he listen to others in this situation? Paul asks the church at Rome to pray for this visit to Jerusalem (see Rom. 15:31). What is ironic about the way in which God answers this prayer?

The commander of the Roman barracks at Jerusalem makes two mistakes.

Firstly, in Acts 21:38, he mistakes Paul for an Egyptian terrorist and assumes he is probably uneducated and unsophisticated, as Egyptians were reputed to be in the first century. Paul is a well-educated, Greek-speaking, Hellenistic Jew.

Secondly, having rescued Paul, he orders him to be flogged in order to extract information from him (v. 24). As in Philippi, so in Jerusalem, the flogging of a Roman citizen was illegal and so Paul calls upon his rights. All Romans had to be treated according to proper legal processes. In Paul's case, this meant that he had to be placed under the jurisdiction of the Sanhedrin. Once again, the commander acts with integrity when his mistake is pointed out to him.

On the steps of the barracks, Paul gives his testimony in Aramaic, the heart language of the people (vv. 1–21). He addresses them respectfully, 'Brothers and fathers' and tells them of his own Jewish heritage and training. In turn, they listen with respect until he says that his ministry is to the Gentiles (v. 21). He asserts that 'The God of our Fathers' (v. 14) has a purpose that includes the Gentiles – the unclean nations, outsiders in His kingdom.

Where now are the thousands who believe and are zealous for the law that we read of in chapter 21? Where now are James and the elders? Paul is left to face the hostility alone. He later testifies that he had been abandoned, but 'the Lord stood at my side and gave me strength' (2 Tim. 4:17). What a sight this must have been – Paul being beaten up by his own countrymen on the steps of the barracks.

Having been beaten, Paul is rescued from the angry crowd and taken to be flogged. We might wonder; will he survive? Will God's plans be thwarted by such aggression? Tension mounts at the end of the chapter, as Paul is brought to appear before the Sanhedrin.

REFLECTION

John Wesley said that parochialism is always the enemy of the gospel.

Why do you think the crowd was so upset in verse 22? Paul is well qualified to reach the Jews (vv. 3,4). What does it tell us about Christian service that God sends him to the Gentiles?

Like Jesus before him (John 18:22), Paul is struck on the face by his opponents. Also like Jesus, it is not apparent why his words should warrant such a response.

Luke is drawing a further contrast between the Roman justice system, which can be trusted and will treat Paul fairly, and the Jewish system, which violates its own law and quickly descends into chaos.

Paul claims that he is being opposed because he maintains the Pharisees' conviction about the resurrection (v. 6). The meeting erupts into further chaos – this time because of the contrary convictions of the Sadducees (v. 8).

Paul is once again rescued, this time in danger of being torn to pieces (v. 10).

Verse 11 contains a wonderfully kind reassurance from God – that no matter how dark things look, Paul will testify in Rome. After all, the word of Ananias is yet to be fulfilled – that Paul will carry Christ's name before the Gentile kings (Acts 9:15).

One wonders how long the forty men mentioned in verses 13 and 14 kept their oath 'not to eat anything until we have killed Paul' (v. 14).

The commander assembles an extraordinary detachment of soldiers to guard Paul (v. 23). Jewish opposition is not underestimated, and Paul's case is treated with the utmost respect by the Roman authorities. The irony is that the Roman pagans become deliverers of God's apostle from the hands of God's ancient people.

The God of the Word is in control. Paul is neither fearful nor uncertain. Paul's perseverance is fed by his trust in God to see His purposes fulfilled. The phrase, 'it must happen' is translated from a little Greek word that is one of the most common words used in Acts (it appears over forty times in Luke–Acts).

Again, the gospel and its messenger prevail in the face of insurmountable odds.

REFLECTION

Acts 23:11 records a direct word from God. Others like this are recorded in Acts 8:26; 9:6,15; 10:19,20; 13:2; 16:9; 18:9,10; 20:22; 27:24. What do these records tell you about the nature of God and His purpose?

Having stood before the crowd in Jerusalem (chapter 22) and before the Sanhedrin (chapter 23), Paul now comes before the Roman tribunal, led by the Roman governor Felix. In Acts, we read that Paul testified before five separate tribunals on his way to Rome. This is the third.

Paul's primary purpose is not to prove his innocence – although that is what transpires – but to persuade his audience of the truth of his experience, and to encourage them to investigate the matter of the resurrection for themselves. (See Acts 24:21; 26:7,8; 26:23; 28:28,29.)

Surely it is Paul's conviction regarding the resurrection of Christ that keeps him going. He makes it clear, when he writes to the Corinthians, that the resurrection of Christ keeps our preaching from being useless (1 Cor. 15:14) our faith from being futile (1 Cor. 15:17) and the believer from being pitied (1 Cor. 15:19). It is because of the resurrection we know that there is life beyond this earthly existence and so, whatever we do for the Lord 'is not in vain' (1 Cor. 15:58).

Paul's and our testifying ministry is never empty, vain or pointless. This is the conviction that gives Paul his persistent focus in every arena, wherever and whenever he speaks.

Drusilla (vv. 24–26) is the daughter of Herod Agrippa I who, earlier in Acts, was recorded as eaten by worms (Acts 12:23). She is Felix's third wife – he persuaded her to leave her husband and join him.

Felix seems to be tantalized by Paul's preaching. Luke tells us he was hoping for the offer of a bribe from Paul (v. 26). Paul's preaching was about righteousness, self-control and judgement (v. 25). Felix and Drusilla needed to realize that if they came to Christ, they couldn't just add Him as an extra to their indulgent lifestyle – instead, they would be fundamentally changed.

REFLECTION

The Jews take the threat of Paul's ministry very seriously. We see this in the naming of their representatives (v. 1), their opening remarks (vv. 2–4) and their charges (vv. 5–8). Why did they treat the case so seriously? Was there any truth in their charges? For other examples of similar charges, see Acts 6:11; 21:21; Luke 23:2.

There is solidarity between the Lord Jesus and His apostles. We see it in the records of Jesus healing a paralytic and then also healing a paralytic through Peter (Acts 3) and Paul (Acts 14).

Also, Jesus raised the dead (Luke 7:11 ff.; 8:51 ff.) and he raises Dorcas through Peter (Acts 9:39 ff.) and the dozing Eutychus through Paul (Acts 20:10).

There is another remarkable parallel going on here, in the record of Paul's trials. Firstly, in Acts 23:27–30, the commander sends a covering letter regarding Paul's case, to Governor Felix. In it, he says there was no charge against Paul that deserved death or imprisonment (Acts 23:29). Secondly, Governor Festus declares before King Agrippa: 'I found he had done nothing deserving of death' (Acts 25:25). Finally, King Agrippa declares of Paul: 'This man is not doing anything that deserves death or imprisonment' (Acts 26:31). Three times, Paul is declared innocent.

In Luke 23, when charges are brought against the Lord Jesus, the Roman governor Pilate says: 'I find no basis for a charge against this man' (v. 4). He repeats this in verse 14 and refers to Herod in verse 15, saying: '... he has done nothing to deserve death.' Three statements of innocence.

All that is happening is under the direct oversight of God. Neither the Lord Jesus, nor His apostolic representative, is tainted by a criminal record. Both have been declared innocent three times.

In Acts 25 Paul defends himself before Festus, Felix's replacement (v. 8), but because he has no confidence that Festus will stand up to the persistence of the Jews, he claims his right as a Roman citizen to appeal to Caesar (v. 11). That right must be respected. In Acts, Paul claims his citizenship rights when, as far as he can see, to do so would be to further the witness of the gospel.

Governor Festus sees in the visit of King Agrippa and his wife, Bernice, an opportunity for advice on Paul's case.

Festus must send a covering letter with Paul to Rome. He would appreciate input from the Herodian king, Agrippa, who is the son of Herod Agrippa I and the brother of Drusilla, mentioned in chapter 24. Agrippa knew the Jewish Scriptures and had the right to appoint the Jewish high priest.

Again, Paul is on the front foot, recounting his testimony for the second time in Acts. Previously he had testified before the crowd in Jerusalem (chapter 22).

Festus interrupts the speech at Paul's mention of the resurrection of the dead (v. 23). In Jerusalem, the crowd had stopped Paul when he claimed the Gentiles would form part of God's people (Acts 22:21). Here, he has already moved past this point of his testimony (vv. 17,18).

On this occasion, the secular Festus stops Paul and doesn't engage in debate (v. 24), but states that Paul is insane because of his insistence on life beyond death. Paul responds by claiming that what he is saying is both 'true and reasonable' (v. 25) and appeals to Agrippa's greater familiarity, as a Jewish leader, with these things.

The gospel will always 'box above its weight'. Aggressive, secular opponents are never a match for Spirit-empowered testimony. We are evidence of that.

Agrippa recognizes Paul's persuasive intent and Paul openly responds – 'pray God that not only you but all who are listening to me today may become what I am' (v. 29).

Paul says in Romans 10:9, 'if you confess with your mouth, "Jesus is Lord," and believe in your heart that God raised him from the dead, you will be saved.'

Here Paul asserts the centrality of the resurrection. This is a word to the closed-minded secularist – 'Why should any of you consider it incredible that God raises the dead?' (v. 8).

REFLECTION

All along the way, Paul's obedience to his calling was costly (Acts 26:16–18). He is compelled by the love of Christ (2 Cor. 5:14,15). Are you compelled in this way? Does your obedience cost you?

'Through many dangers, toils and snares...' having faced court charges, opposition and riots, Paul now faces a natural catastrophe.

Paul and his companions join a ship sailing to Italy, under the oversight of the centurion, Julius. It was late in the sailing season, and becoming dangerous to travel (v. 9). Paul warns about the danger awaiting them, but is disregarded. Instead, Julius listens to the owner of the ship and sails on (vv. 10,11).

A great storm hits and the ship takes a violent battering. Luke, the eyewitness, says, 'we finally gave up all hope of being saved' (v. 20).

Paul now takes the lead. God has spoken to him directly in Acts 18:9,10 and 23:11. Now, an angel appears to him (v. 23). Paul's words are hazy on the detail, but he confidently reassures all those on board that the ship will run aground (v. 26) and that none will be lost. They must stay with the ship in order to be saved (v. 31).

Luke tells us the exact number of people on board – 276 (v. 37) and records that the ship is wrecked (v. 41). All on board are kept safe (vv. 43,44).

There is a parallel and a contrast between these events and the experience of Jonah. Jonah is disobedient towards God, but Paul is obedient to the Word of God. Jonah escapes to sea, but Paul takes to sea. Jonah knows the only hope is for him to leave the ship, and the others on board reluctantly throw him in to the sea. In contrast, Paul knows the only hope is for all to stay on board; his companions are reluctant to do so and try to abandon ship (v. 30). We see a parallel in that ultimately, the compliance of Jonah's and Paul's fellow travellers ensures their safety in both cases.

No raging tempest can thwart God's plan – not even the murderous intent of the soldiers (v. 42), thwarted by Julius (v. 43).

As the events unfold, Julius's leadership recedes as Paul's becomes more dominant.

John Newton began his career as a sailor on board his father's merchant ship in these same waters of the Mediterranean. On 10 May 1748, he captained a slave ship struck by a great storm off the coast of Africa. He later wrote of this experience in the hymn 'Amazing Grace', perhaps recalling Paul's experience in Acts 27:

Through many dangers, toils and snares
I have already come:
'Tis grace has brought me safe thus far,
And grace will lead me home.[16]

REFLECTION

In what ways does Acts 27:25 reveal the key to Paul's steadfastness? Compare and contrast Paul's demeanour with that of the sailors and the soldiers on board the ship.

Paul arrives on Malta, where Luke records that he and his companions are shown 'unusual kindness' (vv. 2; also v. 10).

Even though he has emerged as the leader of the sailing party, Paul is not above ordinary tasks, such as collecting firewood (v. 3).

A snake bites Paul, and the Maltese conclude he must be a murderer, because he has survived the storm, only to die of snakebite. When Paul does not die, the consensus changes and he is thought to be a god. The people venerate him, just as the Lystrans did in Acts 14:11. In the record of this incident of the snakebite, Paul's solidarity with Jesus and His messengers is reinforced. (See Luke 10:19.)

Paul has an active ministry on Malta – further evidence of his ministry to Greeks and non-Greeks (see Rom. 1:14). After three months there, they continue the journey to Rome (Acts 28:11–14).

The ship that brought Paul to Puteoli, the seaport of Rome, sailed under the figurehead of Castor and Pollux on its bow (v. 11). These were the mythical twin sons of Zeus, thought to be protectors of those who sail upon the seas. But Paul's deliverer all through *his* journey has been Yahweh. Paul now arrives on the coast of Italy under the figurehead of these pagan deities, but his encouragement does not come from these brothers. On the contrary, Luke writes in verse 14, 'There we found some brothers ...' Also at Rome, 'The brothers there ... travelled ... to meet us' (v. 15). Paul was thankful and encouraged by the members of the family of the true God.

Emotionally and physically exhausted as he was, Paul took great heart at the sight of these brothers in Christ, in preparation for whatever awaited him in his appeal to Caesar.

REFLECTION

Paul has come through an exhausting storm and shipwreck, been washed up on a beach, bitten by a viper, and now he is about to walk from Puteoli to Rome (140 miles). God's gospel is unstoppable and its messenger, who still has work to do, is also unstoppable. How do these facts affect the way you think about:

- *your life;*
- *your ministry;*
- *your mission?*

One of the features of Luke's writing is the significance he attaches to last words. For example, in the introduction to his Gospel (Luke 1:1–4) where he addresses Theophilus, the last word in the Greek text, where Luke wants the emphasis to fall, is 'certainty'. He wants Theophilus to have certainty.

In the Greek text of Acts, the last word is the word 'unhinderedly' (v. 31). This adverb is used to qualify the participles 'proclaiming' and 'teaching'. Luke wants to emphasize that the proclamation and teaching of the Word of God continues unhinderedly.

The Word of God has come to Rome. We know from Romans 15:20 ff. that Paul's ambition was to take the gospel where Christ is not known – to take it as far west as he thought he could go, to Spain (Rom. 15:24).

Paul makes it clear that he bears no ill will towards his own people. Rather, it is because of his steadfast commitment to 'the hope of Israel' that he is in chains (v. 20).

The brothers at Rome have not received any bad reports against Paul (v. 21). However, they know that many people are speaking against the Christian sect (v. 22).

The consistency of Paul's persuasive ministry (v. 23) is matched by the Jews consistently obstinate response (vv. 24,25). Paul warns them about a hardened non-response to the gospel (vv. 26,27).

Here, at the end of Acts, the gospel has reached Rome as God said it would. Did Paul make his appeal to Caesar? Was he released? Did he get to Spain?

Luke has reached the objective of his history by bringing Paul to Rome, where he enjoys complete liberty to preach the gospel, under the eyes of the imperial guard. The programme mapped out in [Acts] 1:8 has been carried through![17]

But at the point where Luke laid down his pen, Paul – though in chains – and the gospel of God's kingly rule were irrepressibly surging ahead without let up or hindrance in spite of human opposition or nature's storms.'[18]

REFLECTION

At the end of his commentary on Acts 1:8, Professor E.M. Blaiklock sums up the book in this way: 'To press beyond the fringe is always sound policy, provided it is done with vigour and devotion.' How does Acts encourage you to press beyond the fringe? Will you do it with vigour and devotion?[19]

REFERENCES

[1] C.H. Spurgeon, quoted in *Reformation & Revival Journal*, vol. 9, no. 1 (Winter 2000).

[2] Matthew Henry, *Commentary on the Whole Bible: Acts to Revelation*, vol. 6 (Mclean, VA: MacDonald Publishing, 1985).

[3] Matthew Henry, *Commentary on the Whole Bible: Acts to Revelation*, vol. 6 (Mclean, VA: MacDonald Publishing, 1985). F.F. Bruce, *Paul: Apostle of the Free Spirit* (Milton Keynes: Paternoster Press, 2004).

[4] Tertullian, quoted in 'Apology' 50.14 (Grand Rapids, MI: Eerdmans, 1992).

[5] John Newton, 1725–1807 *Olney Hymns*.

[6] Campbell Morgan, *The Acts of the Apostles* (NY: F.H. Revell Co., 1924).

[7] F.F. Bruce, *Paul: Apostle of the Free Spirit* (Carlisle: Paternoster Press, 1992).

[8] B. Pascal, *Pensées; Selections* (London: SCM Press Ltd., 1959).

[9] John Newton quoted in John Stott, *Acts: Seeing the Spirit at Work* (Nottingham: IVP, 2008), pp. 67.

[10] D.M. Lloyd-Jones, *Preaching and Preachers*, (Grand Rapids, MI: Zondervan, 1972), p.130.

[11] C.H. Spurgeon, *Lectures to My Students* (Grand Rapids, MI: Zondervan, 1980), p. 7.

[12] Augustine, Epistle 21:4

[13] E.M. Blaiklock, 'Commentary on The Acts of the Apostles', *Tyndale New Testament Commentaries* (London: Tyndale, IVP, 1959), p. 172.

[14] John Calvin, *Synoptic Gospels*, II:159.

[15] John Calvin, *Acts*, I:381.

[16] 'Amazing Grace', John Newton (1725–1807)

[17] F.F. Bruce, *Commentary on the Greek Text of Acts* (Grand Rapids, MI: Eerdmans, 1988), p. 543.

[18] David Gooding, *True to the Faith* (Gospel Folio), p. 371.

[19] E.M. Blaiklock, 'Commentary on The Acts of the Apostles', *Tyndale New Testament Commentaries* (London: Tyndale, IVP, 1959), p. 50.

MORE IN THIS SERIES

ROMANS: Momentous News
By David Cook
ISBN: 978-1-906173-24-1

MARK: The Suffering Servant
By Jeremy McQuoid
ISBN: 978-1-906173-55-5

1 THESSALONIANS: Living for Jesus
By Julia Marsden
ISBN: 978-1-906173-67-8

DANIEL: Far From Home
By Justin Mote
ISBN: 978-1-906173-68-5

10 Publishing
a division of **10**ofthose.com

To place an order call: **0844 879 3243** email: **sales@10ofthose.com**
or order online: **www.10ofthose.com**

a division of 10 of those.com

10Publishing is the publishing house of 10ofThose.
It is committed to producing quality Christian
resources that are biblical and accessible.

www.10ofthose.com is our online retail arm selling
thousands of quality books at discounted prices.
We also service many church bookstalls
and can help your church to set up a bookstall.
Single and bulk purchases welcome.

For information contact: sales@10ofthose.com
or check out our website: www.10ofthose.com